FULL THROTTLE

HOT RODS

BY THOMAS K. ADAMSON

EPIC

BELLWETHER MEDIA • MINNEAPOLIS, MN

EPIC BOOKS are no ordinary books. They burst with intense action, high-speed heroics, and shadows of the unknown. Are you ready for an Epic adventure?

This edition first published in 2019 by Bellwether Media, Inc.

No part of this publication may be reproduced in whole or in part without written permission of the publisher. For information regarding permission, write to Bellwether Media, Inc., Attention: Permissions Department, 6012 Blue Circle Drive, Minnetonka, MN 55343.

Library of Congress Cataloging-in-Publication Data

Names: Adamson, Thomas K., 1970- author.
Title: Hot Rods / by Thomas K. Adamson.
Other titles: Hot Rods (Bellwether Media)
Description: Minneapolis, MN : Bellwether Media, Inc., 2019. | Series: Epic. Full Throttle | Includes bibliographical references and index.
Identifiers: LCCN 2018002179 (print) | LCCN 2018017750 (ebook) | ISBN 9781681036199 (ebook) | ISBN 9781626178724 (hardcover : alk. paper)
Subjects: LCSH: Hot rods–Juvenile literature. | Off-road vehicles–Juvenile literature.
Classification: LCC TL236.3 (ebook) | LCC TL236.3 .A2422 2019 (print) | DDC 629.228/6–dc23
LC record available at https://lccn.loc.gov/2018002179

Editor: Christina Leaf   Designer: Jeffrey Kollock

Printed in the United States of America, North Mankato, MN

TABLE OF CONTENTS

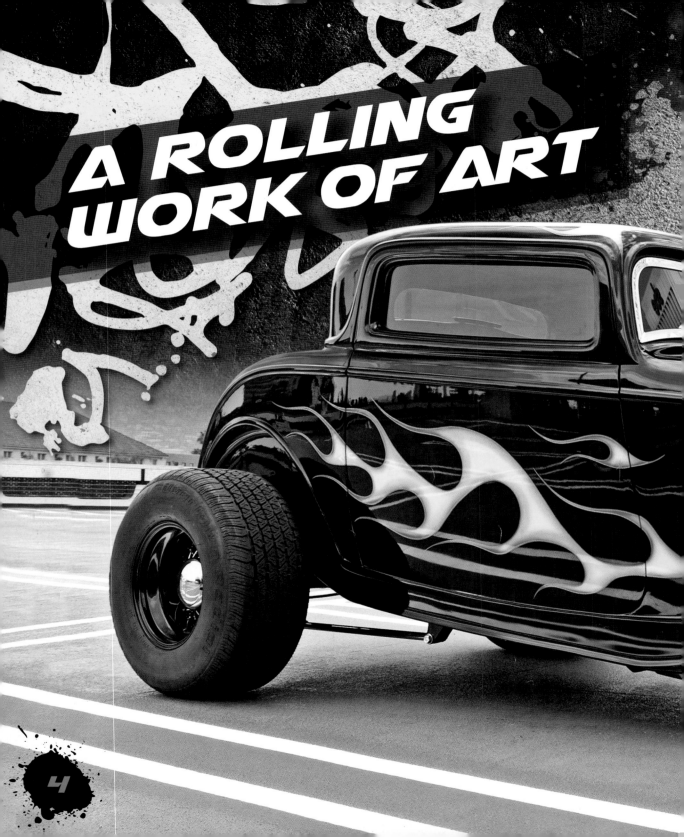

A ROLLING WORK OF ART

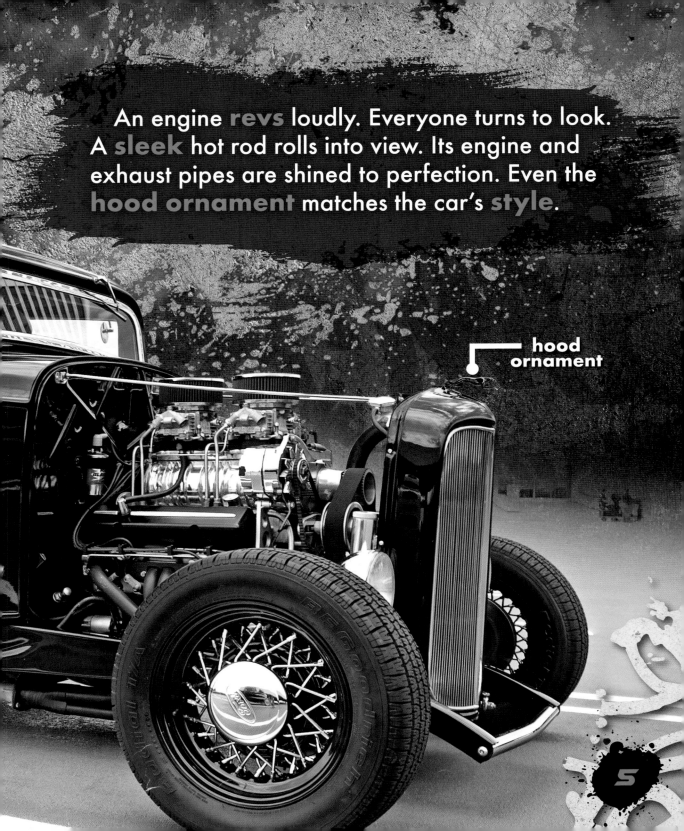

An engine **revs** loudly. Everyone turns to look. A **sleek** hot rod rolls into view. Its engine and exhaust pipes are shined to perfection. Even the **hood ornament** matches the car's **style**.

hood ornament

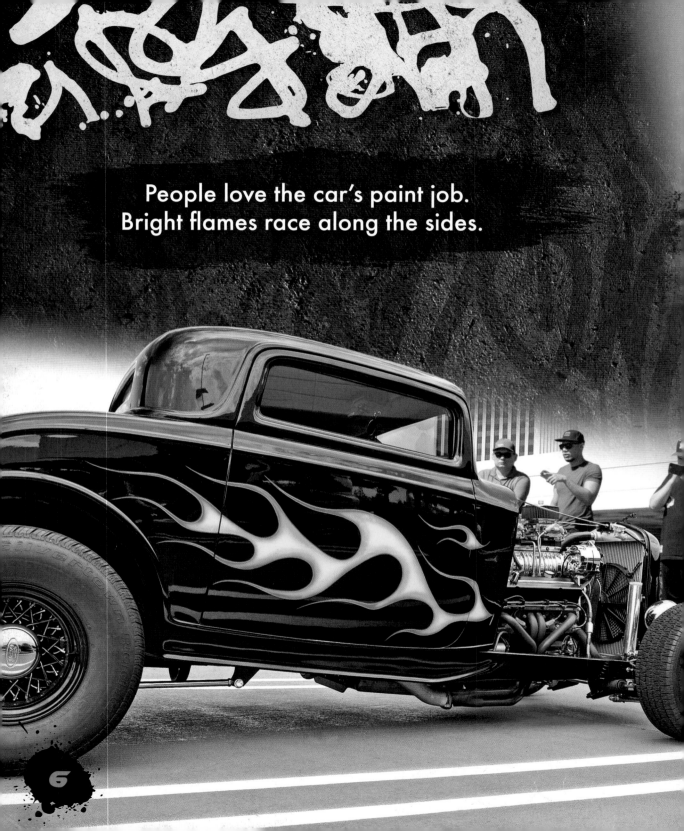

People love the car's paint job.
Bright flames race along the sides.

6

Nearby, other hot rods show off their designs. Hot rods are rolling works of art!

WHAT ARE HOT RODS?

Hot rods are old cars rebuilt to look cool or to go fast. These awesome cars are for people who love to **tinker**. They show off their owners' style and **mechanical** skill.

BREAKING THE LAW

Hot rods were once used for illegal street racing. Other hot rodders raced on dry lakebeds in California.

At car shows, people can see
a hot rod's polished look up close.

Some hot rodders take their cars to the streets.
They show off their engine work in races.

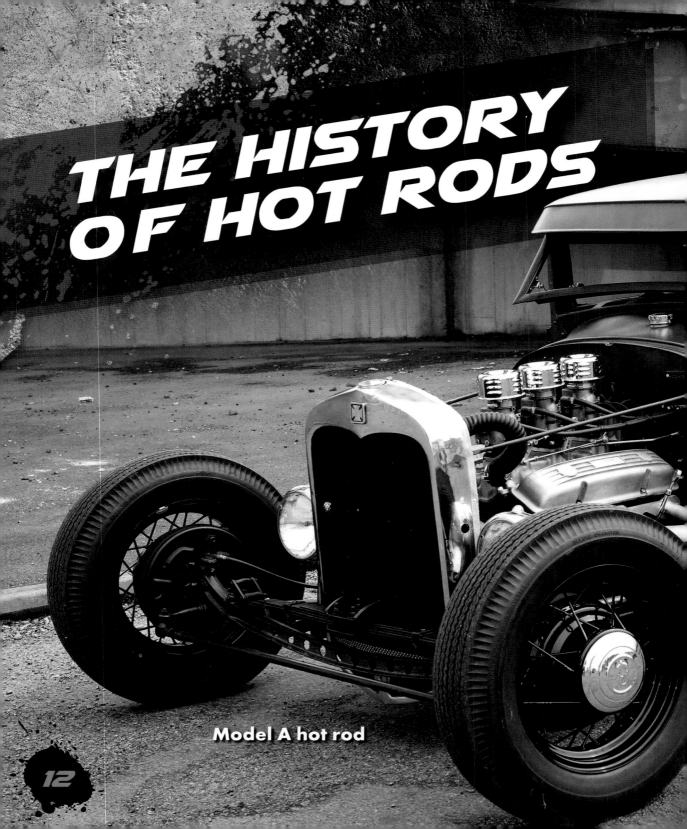

THE HISTORY OF HOT RODS

Model A hot rod

CRUISING

Hot rods became even more popular in the 1950s. Teens and young adults cruised the streets to show off their cars.

In the 1920s and 1930s, people with little money still wanted fast, stylish cars. Model T and Model A Fords were common and cheap. Parts were easy to find. People fixed these up to make cooler cars.

HOT ROD TIMELINE

1951

National Hot Rod Association is founded to promote safety

1948

Hot Rod magazine is established

HOT ROD

PICTORIAL

Testing and Servicing
TURN SIGNALS
and
GAUGES

COMBUSTION

LATE 1940s

Hot rods become more popular when World War II soldiers return and take an interest in cars

14

1970

The first Street Rod Nationals takes place, and the National Street Rod Association (NSRA) forms

1983

Goodguys Rod and Custom Association is established to promote hot rod events

People liked tinkering with their hot rods. They took off the fenders, hood, and top to make them lighter. They made the engine more powerful. Fake pipes and fancy **hubcaps** made them look

HOT ROD PARTS

Today, hot rodders love to show off their cars' **souped-up** engines. Pipes and hoses are kept perfectly clean. Some engine parts are plated with **chrome** for extra shine. Many paint the engine, too.

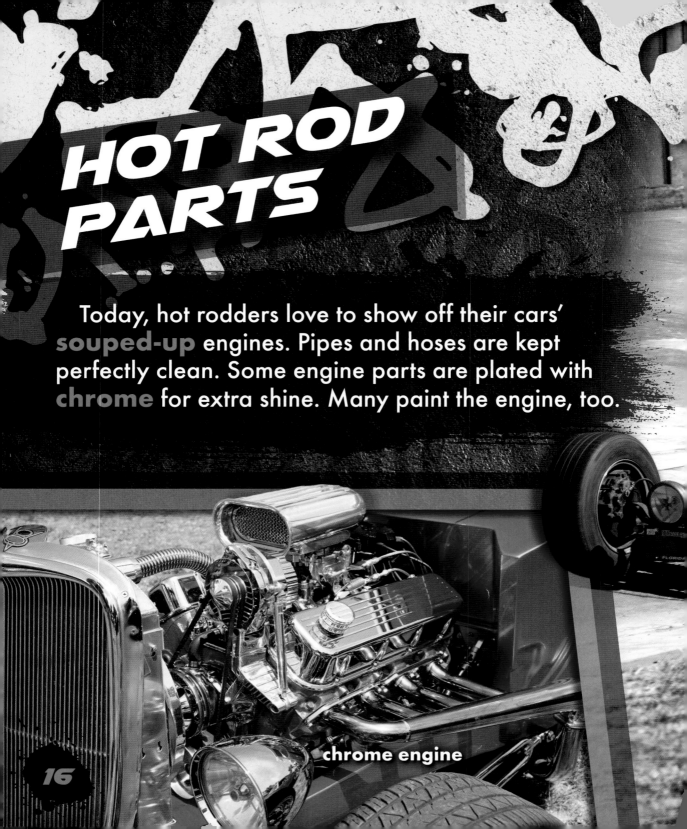

chrome engine

16

rat rod

RAT RODS

Some hot rods, called rat rods, may be dull colors, rusty, or dented. Owners prefer original parts to new or custom-made ones.

17

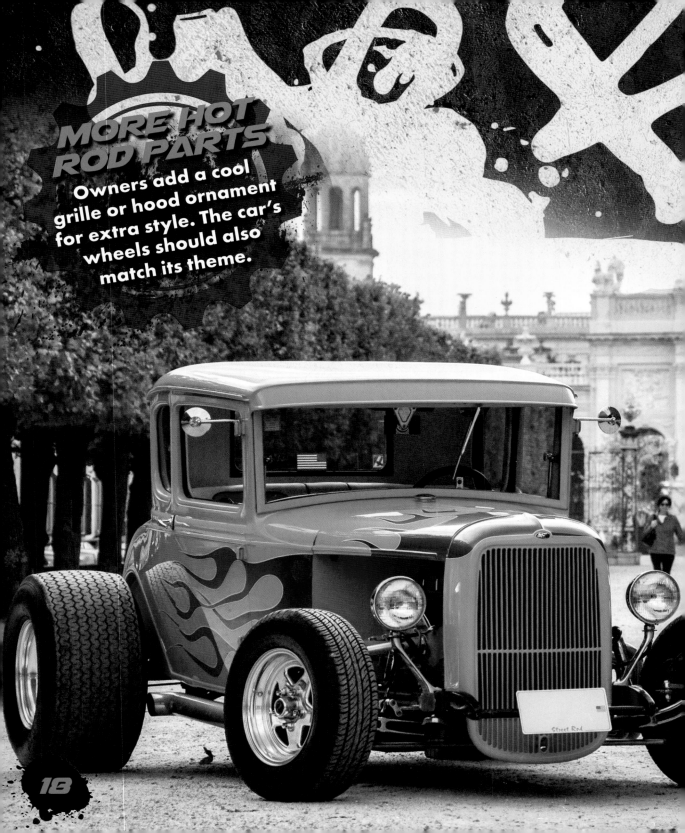

MORE HOT ROD PARTS

Owners add a cool grille or hood ornament for extra style. The car's wheels should also match its theme.

A great paint job makes a hot rod look unique. Bright colors and flames are popular. **Chopping** makes the hot rod look sleek and smooth. Early hot rodders did this to make the car faster.

IDENTIFY A HOT ROD

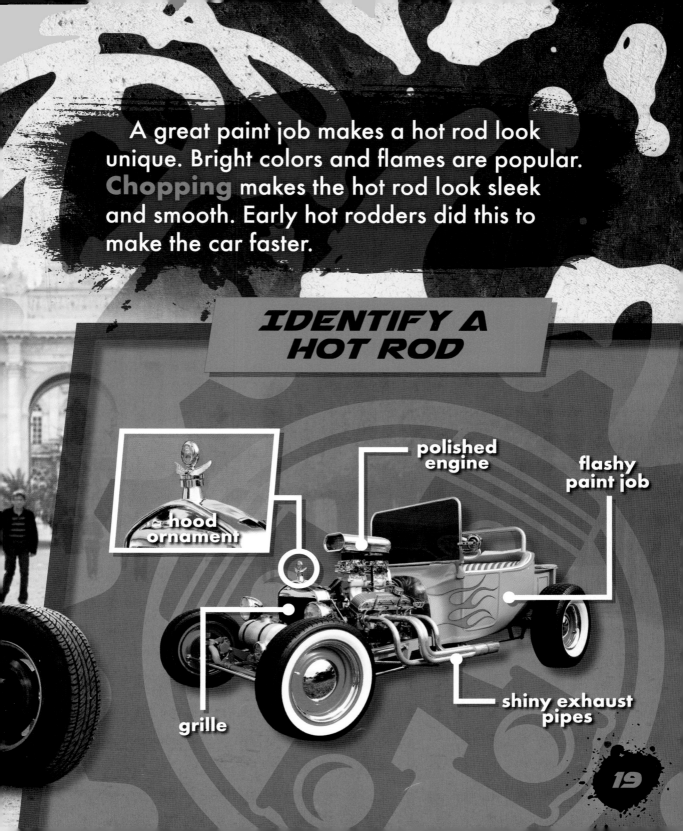

hood ornament

polished engine

flashy paint job

grille

shiny exhaust pipes

HOT ROD COMPETITIONS

drag race

At car shows, hot rods win awards for style and creativity. In other contests, winding courses test a hot rod's **suspension** and handling. **Drag races** test the car's speed. Hot rods are the coolest cars on the street!

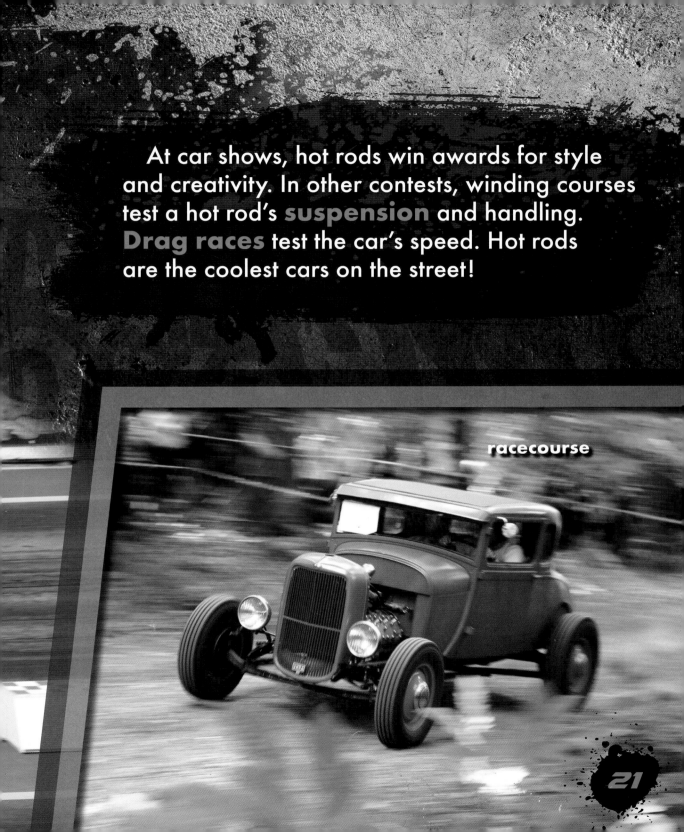

racecourse

GLOSSARY

chopping—cutting off part of the top of a hot rod to lower the roof and make it look more sleek

chrome—a shiny silver metal used as a protective covering or for decoration

drag races—short, fast races between two cars on a straight track

hood ornament—a small metal figure on the front of a car's hood

hubcaps—metal caps that cover the side of wheels

mechanical—having to do with machines or engines

revs—increases in speed; the engine gets louder when it revs.

sleek—smooth and polished

souped-up—increased in power or appeal

style—a way of expressing oneself

suspension—the system of springs, tires, and shocks that cushions a vehicle's ride

tinker—to make small adjustments or repairs

TO LEARN MORE

AT THE LIBRARY

Lanier, Wendy Hinote. *Hot Rods*. Lake Elmo, Minn.:
North Star Editions, 2017.

Westcott, Jim. *Performance Cars*. Mankato, Minn.:
Black Rabbit Books, 2018.

Willson, Quentin. *Cool Cars*. New York, N.Y.:
DK Publishing, 2014.

ON THE WEB

Learning more about hot rods
is as easy as 1, 2, 3.

1. Go to www.factsurfer.com.

2. Enter "hot rods" into the search box.

3. Click the "Surf" button and you will see a list
   of related web sites.

With factsurfer.com, finding more information
is just a click away.

INDEX

The images in this book are reproduced through the courtesy of: betto rodrigues, front cover, p. 1; Philip Pilosian, pp. 4-5, 6; Richard Thornton, p. 7; Christ Phutully/ Creative Commons, p. 8; NSC Photography, p. 9 (car); zhu difeng, p. 9 (background); Sean Donohue Photo, p. 10; imageBROKER/ Alamy, p. 11; Ian Shipley Auto/ Alamy, pp. 12-13; amophoto_au, pp. 14-15; Hot Rod Magazine/ Flickr, p. 14 (magazine cover); Racing One/ Getty Images, p. 14 (1940s); Steve Lagreca, p. 15; Carolo7, p. 16; attila, pp. 16-17; Alexandre Prévot/ Flickr, pp. 18-19; Images-USA/ Alamy, p. 19; Manfred Steinbach, pp. 20-21; Michael Johnson/ Alamy, p. 21.